Uppercase Letter Tracing Workbook

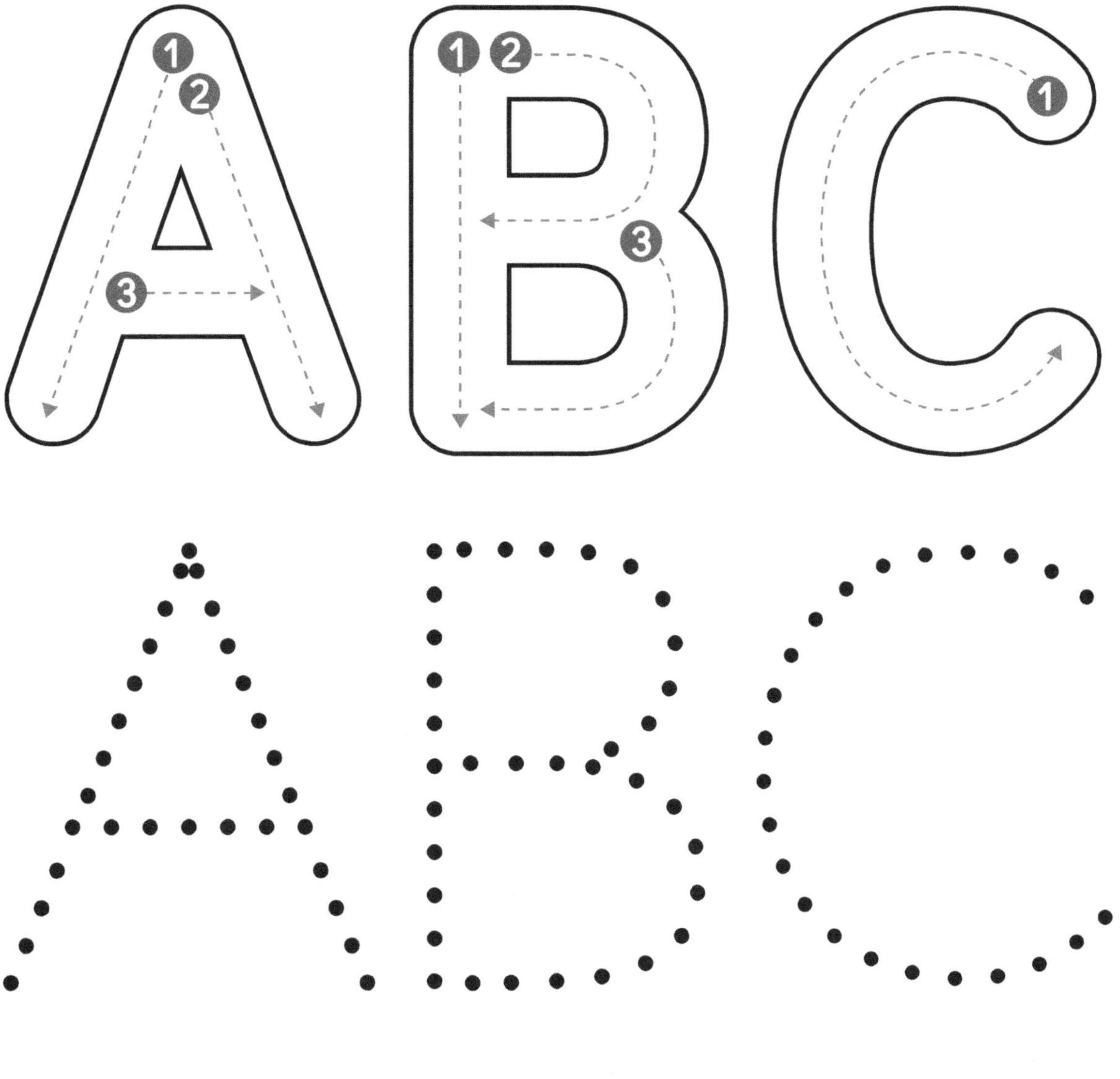

_____

Write your name above.

Let's get started!

Finger trace the letter

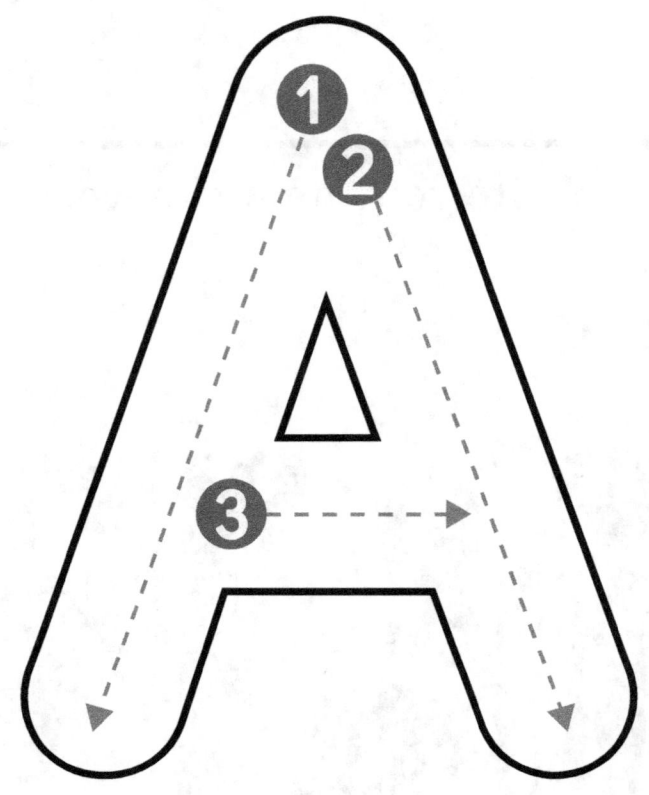

Trace the letters

Finger trace the letter

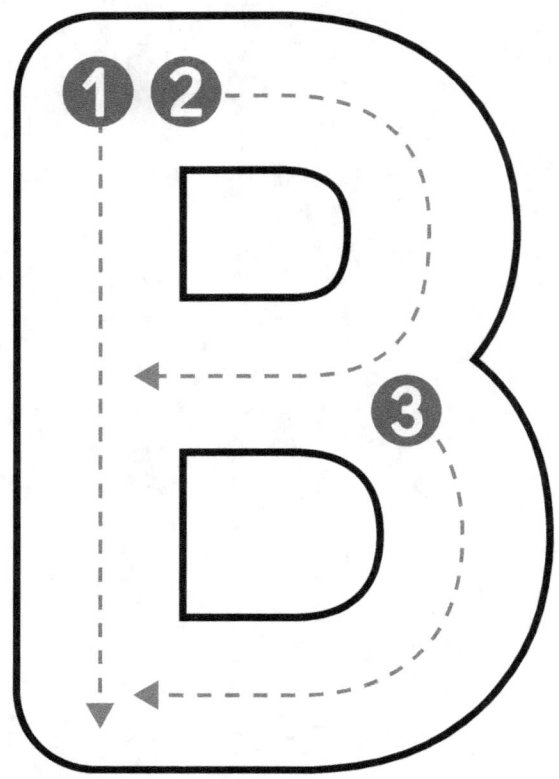

Trace the letters

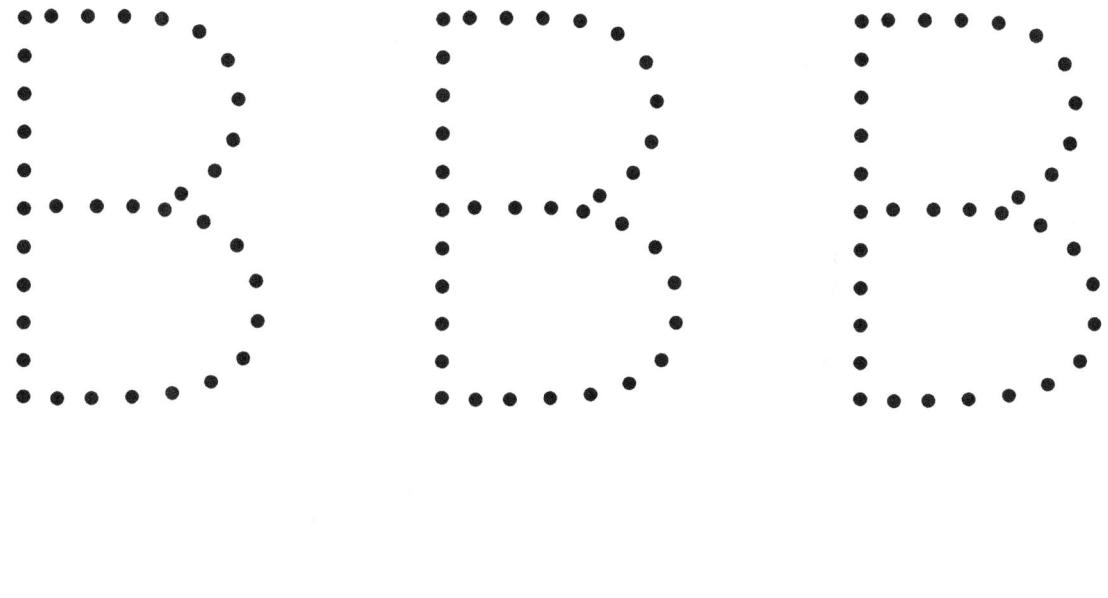

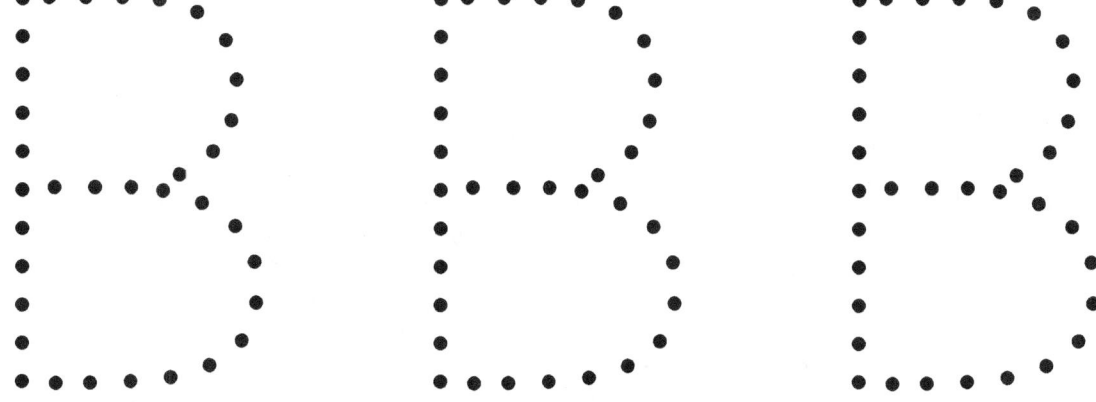

Finger trace the letter

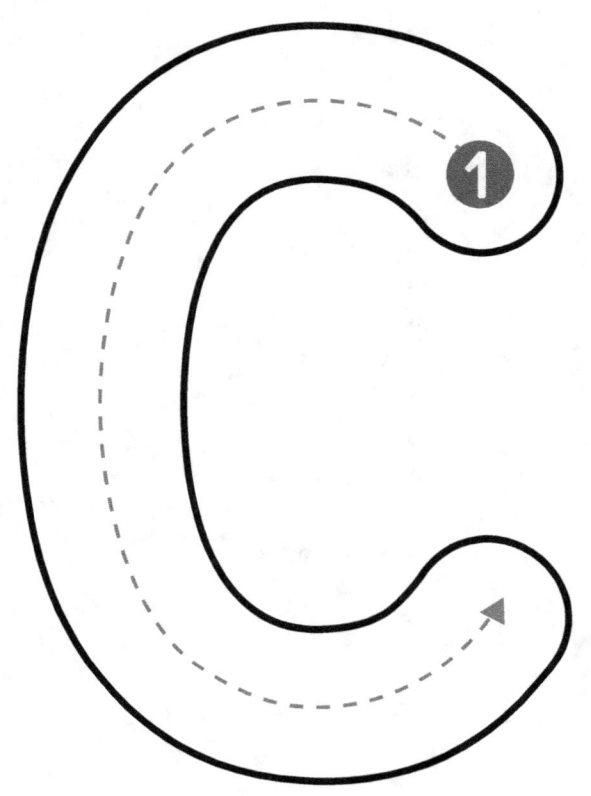

Trace the letters

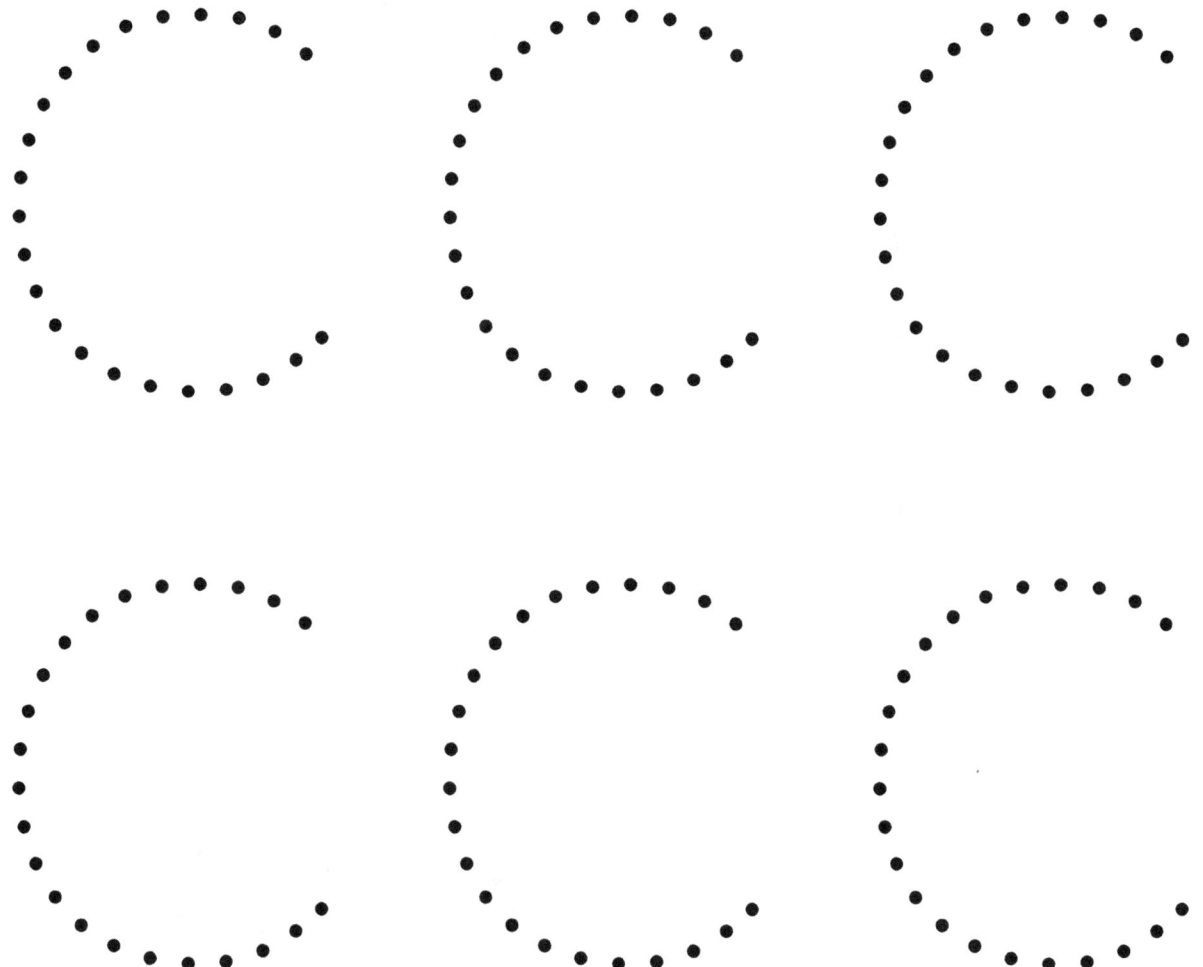

Finger trace the letter

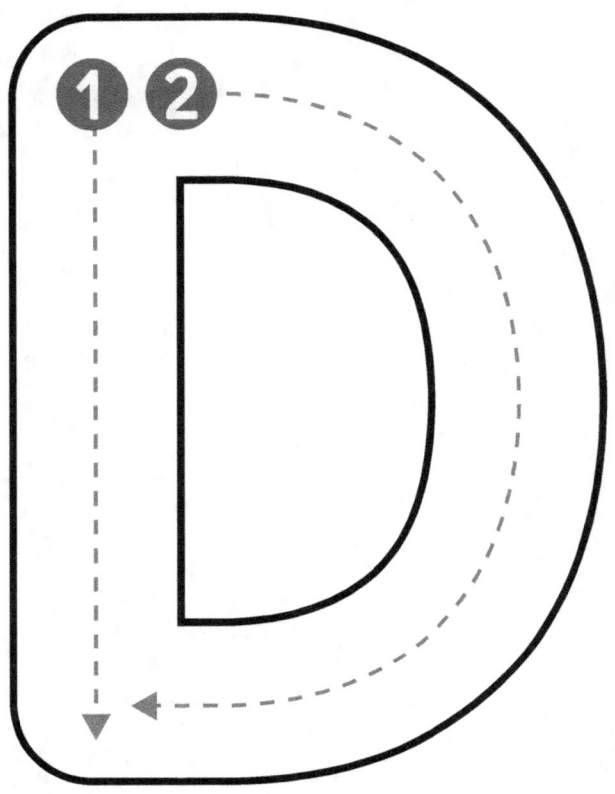

Trace the letters

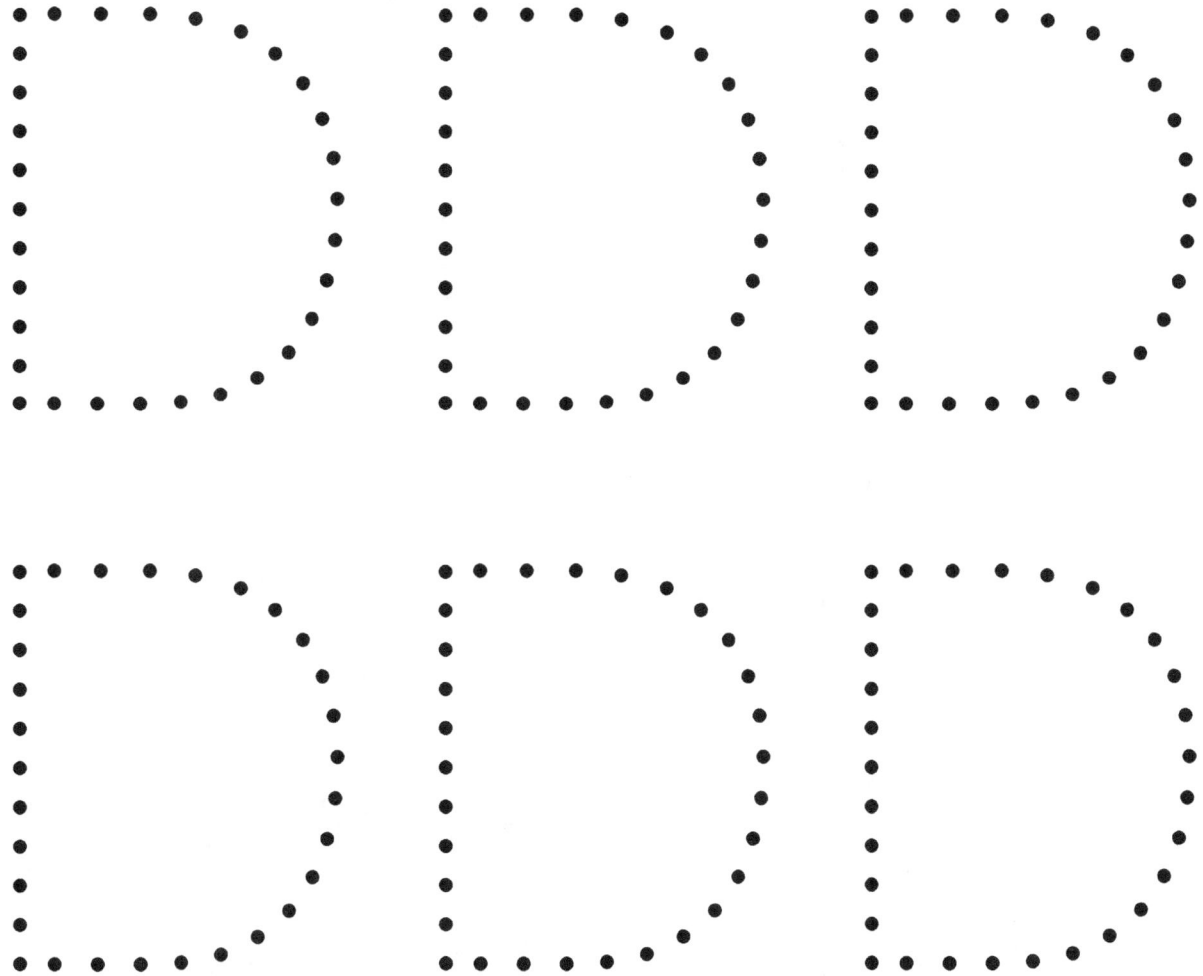

Finger trace the letter

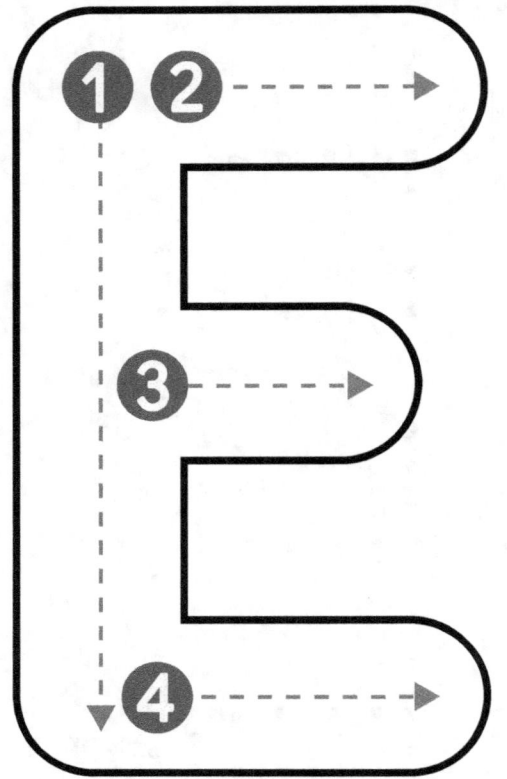

Trace the letters

Finger trace the letter

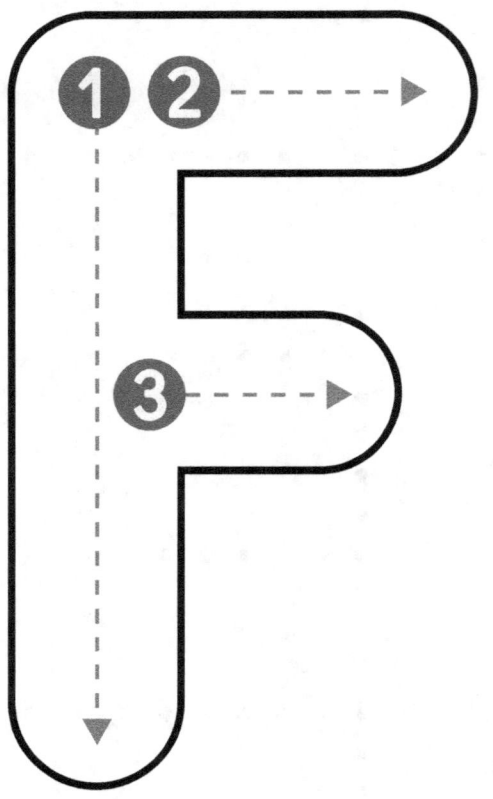

Trace the letters

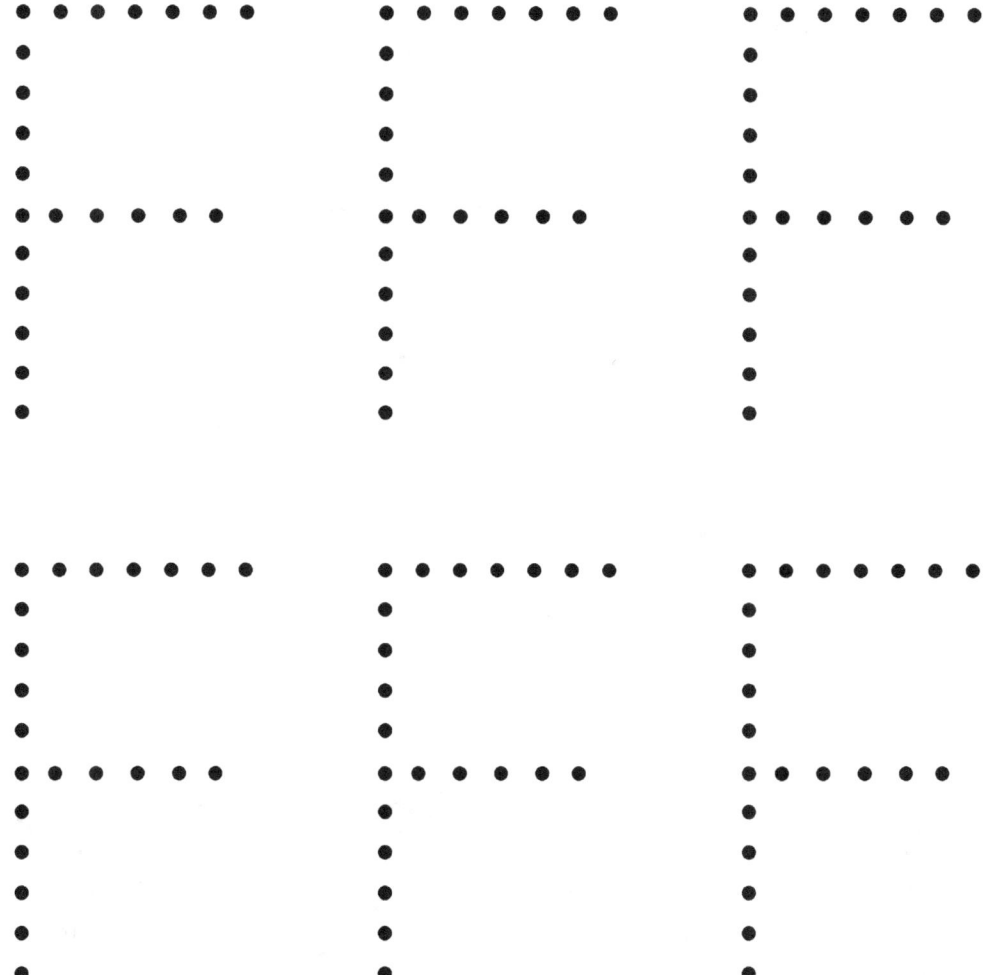

Finger trace the letter

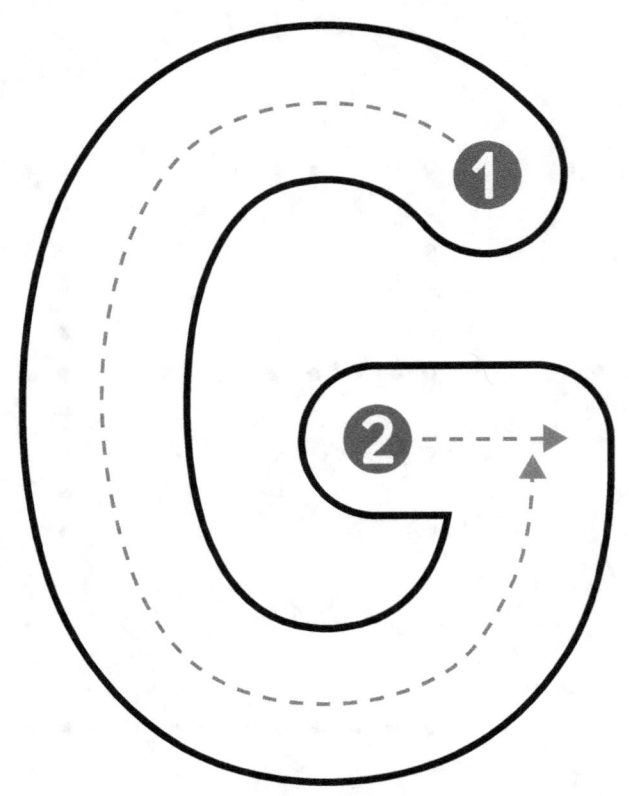

Trace the letters

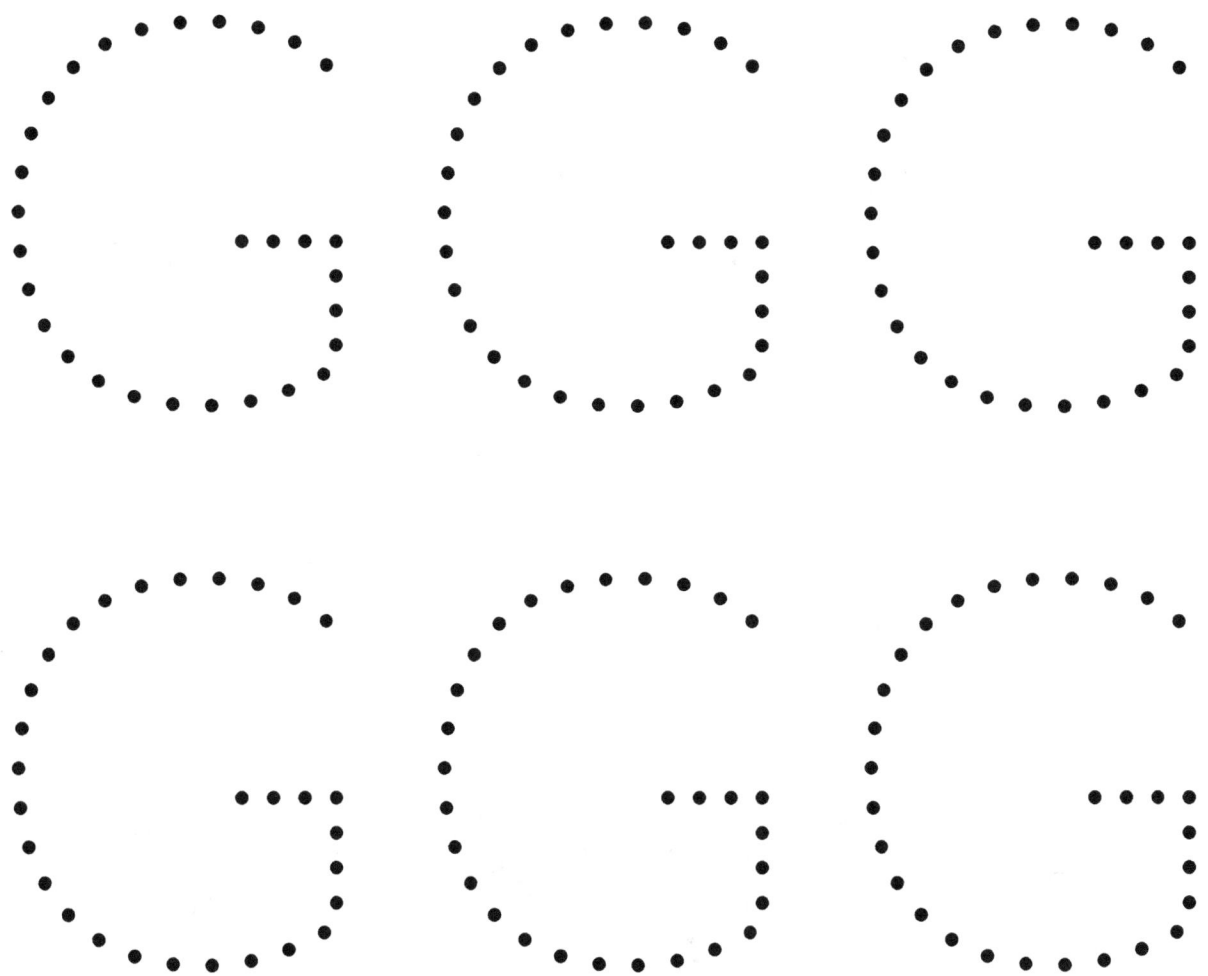

Finger trace the letter

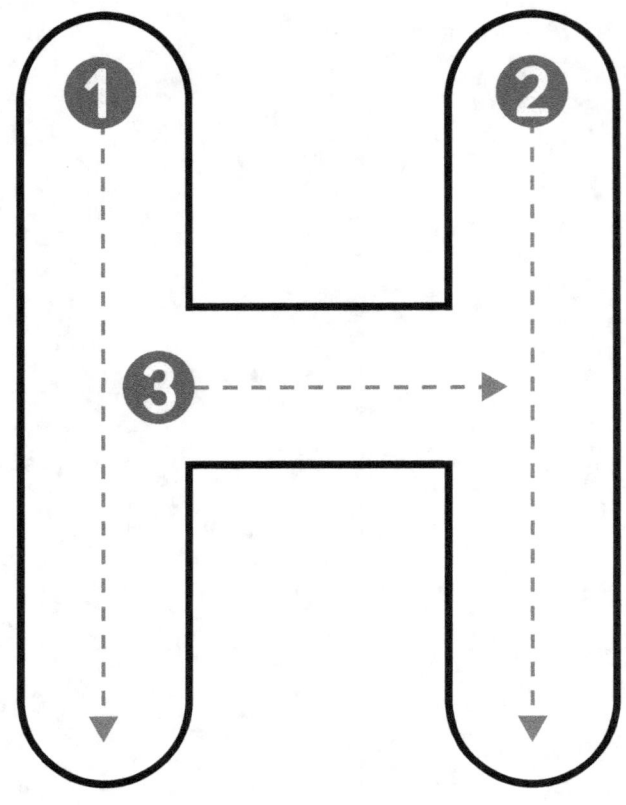

Trace the letters

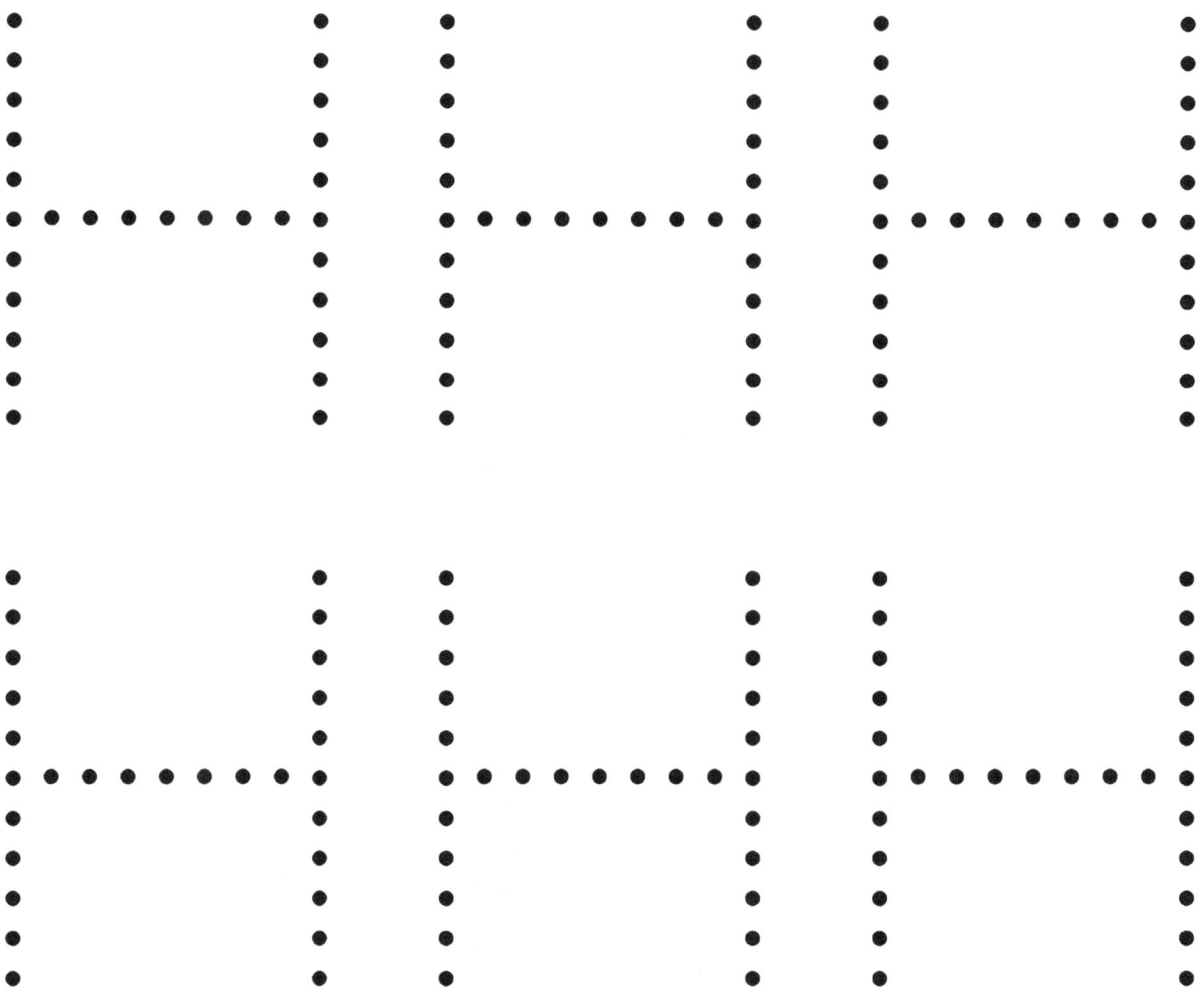

Finger trace the letter

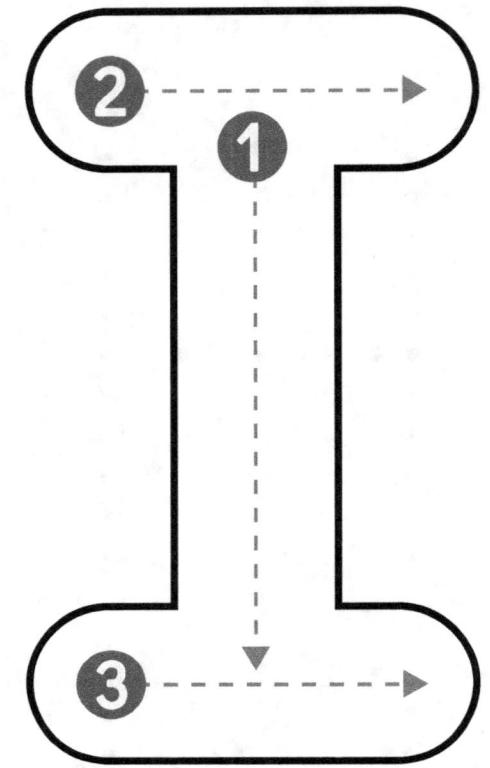

Trace the letters

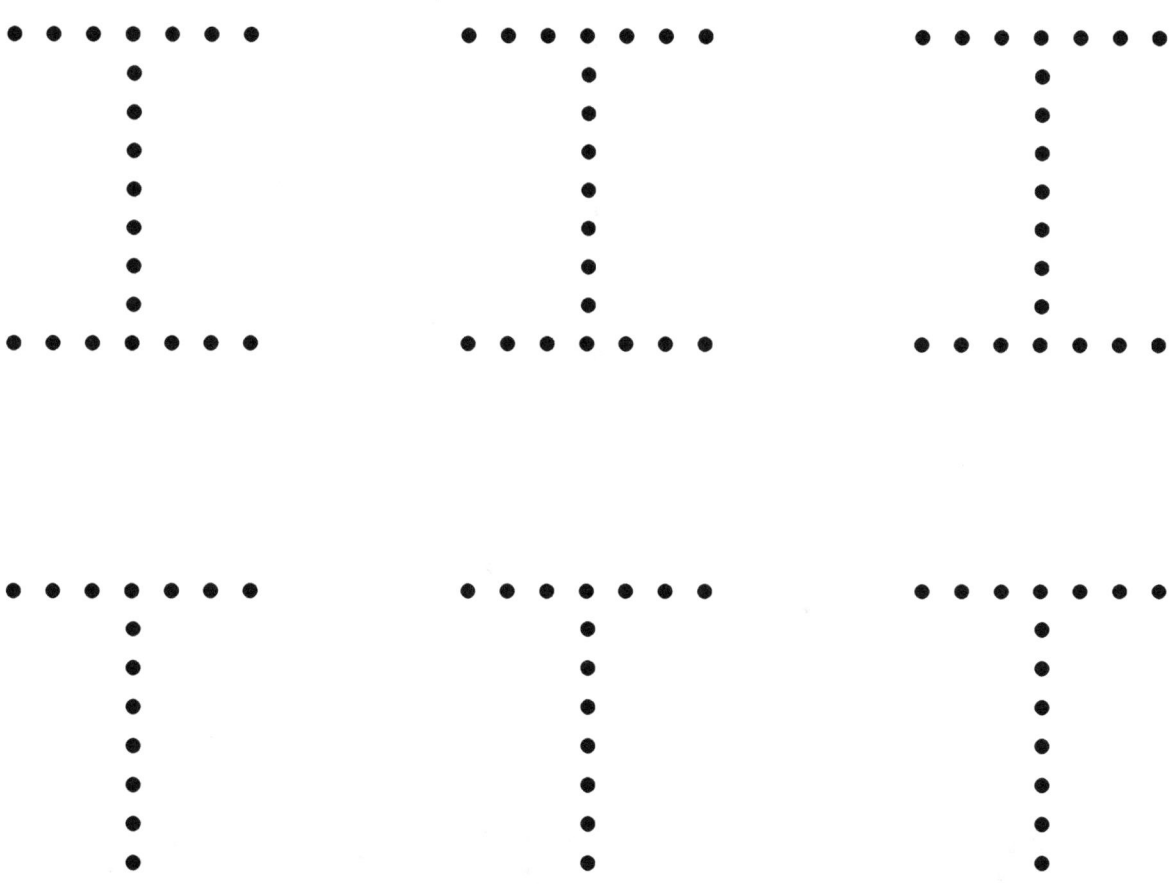

Finger trace the letter

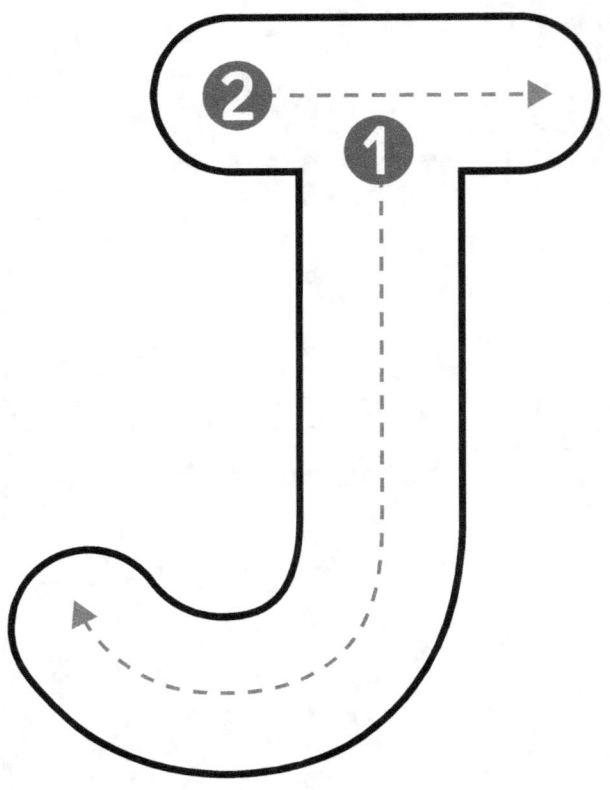

Trace the letters

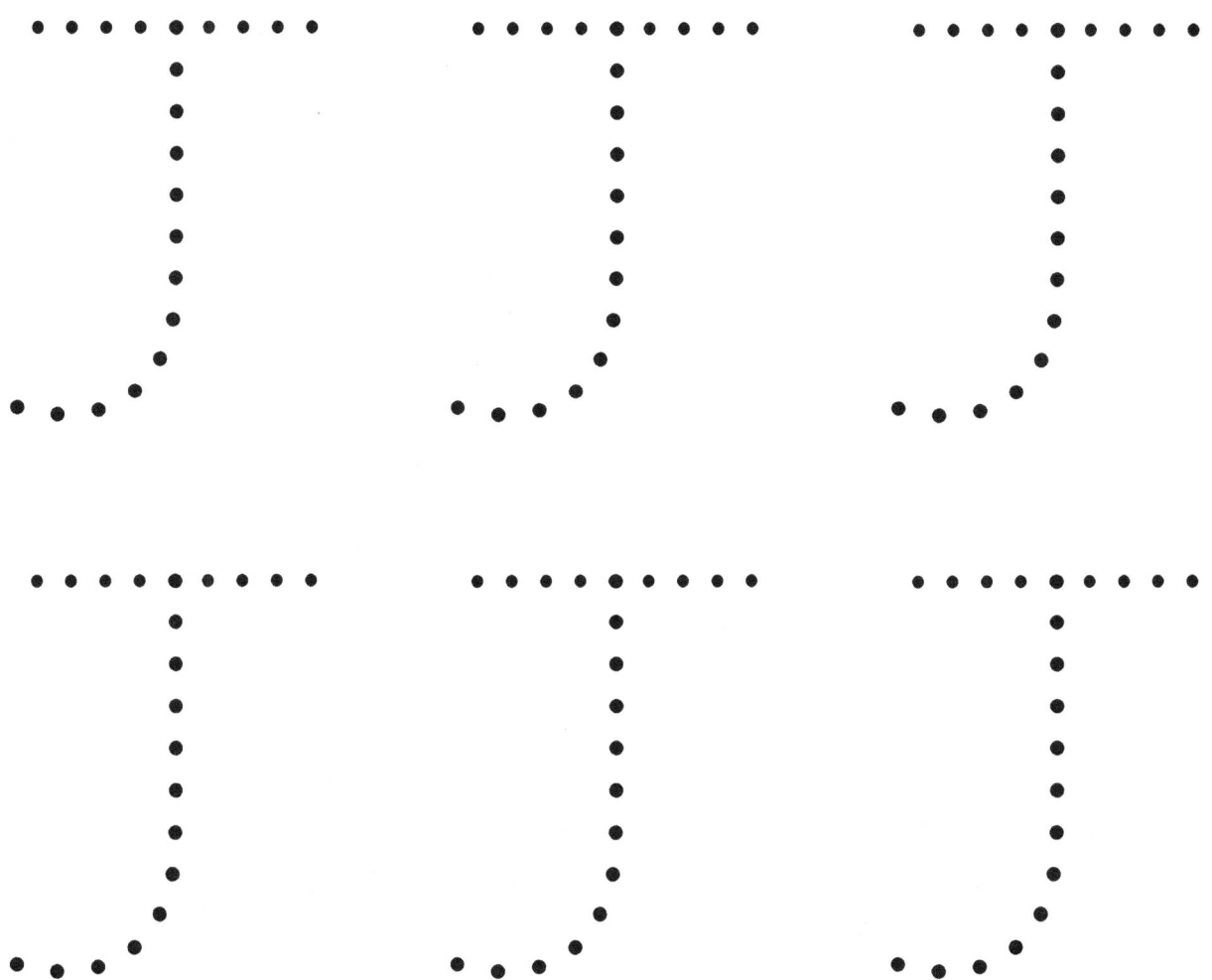

Finger trace the letter

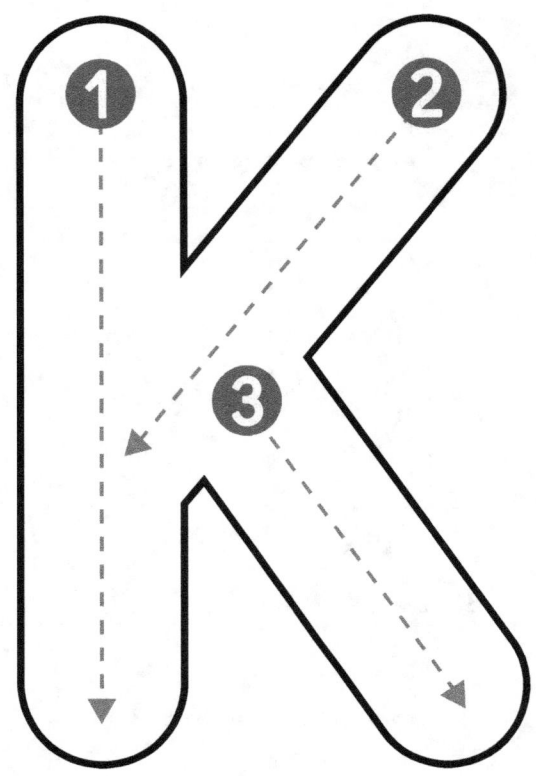

Trace the letters

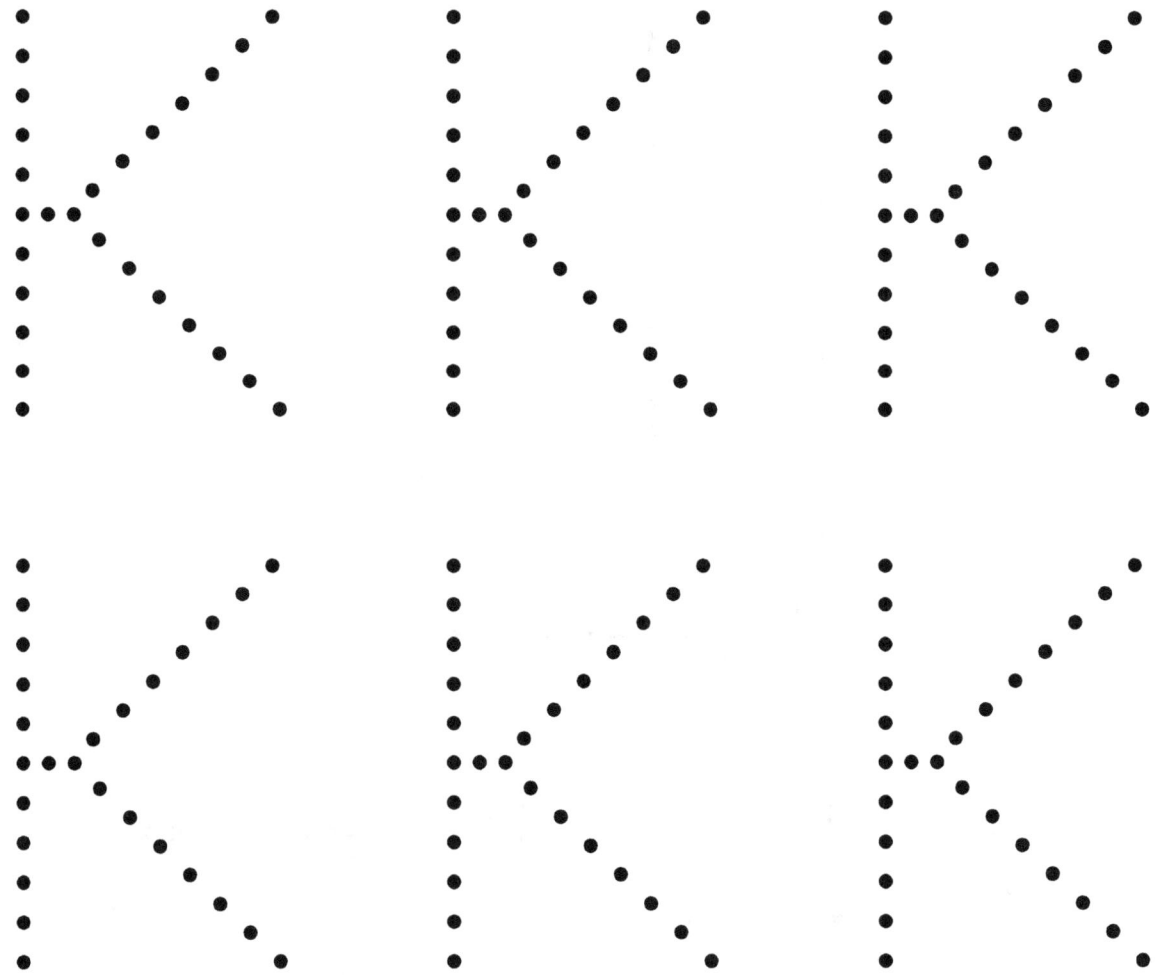

Finger trace the letter

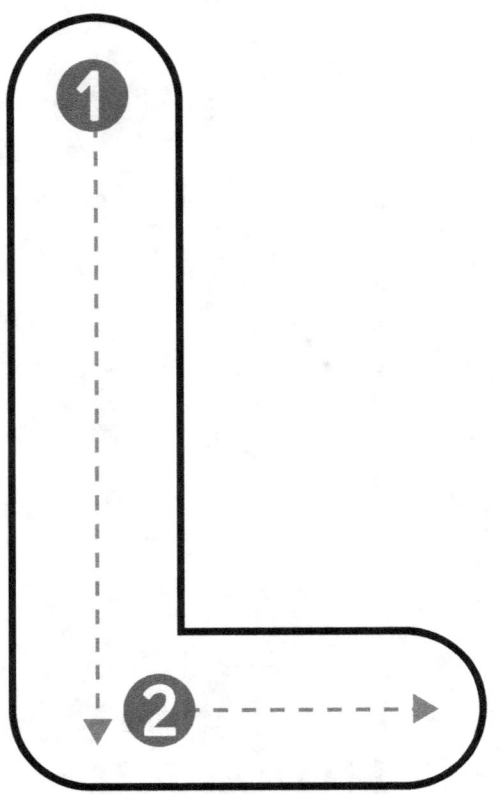

Trace the letters

Finger trace the letter

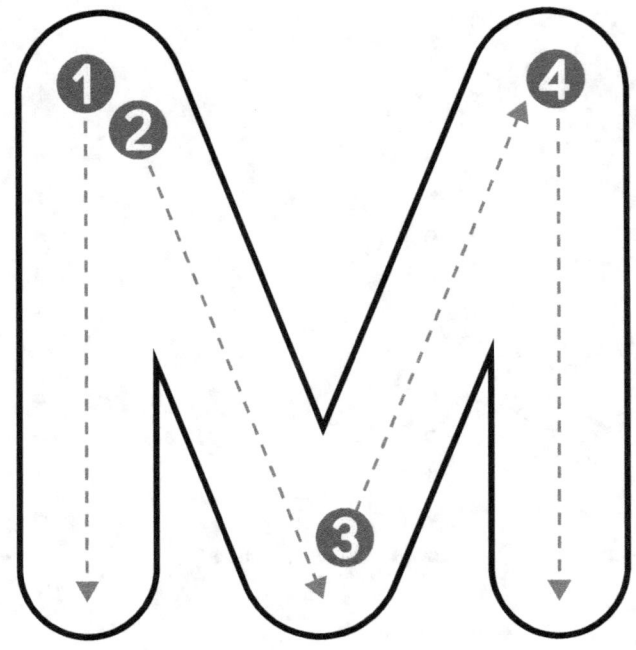

Trace the letters

Finger trace the letter

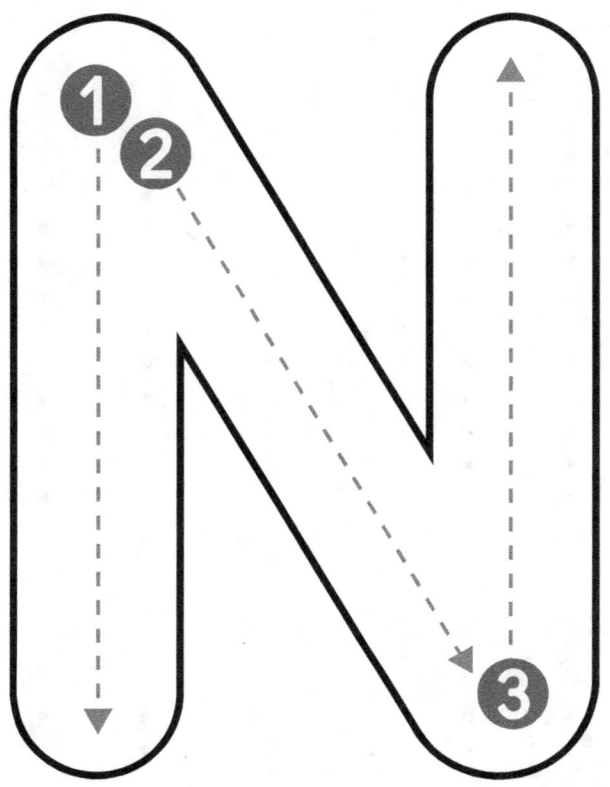

Trace the letters

Finger trace the letter

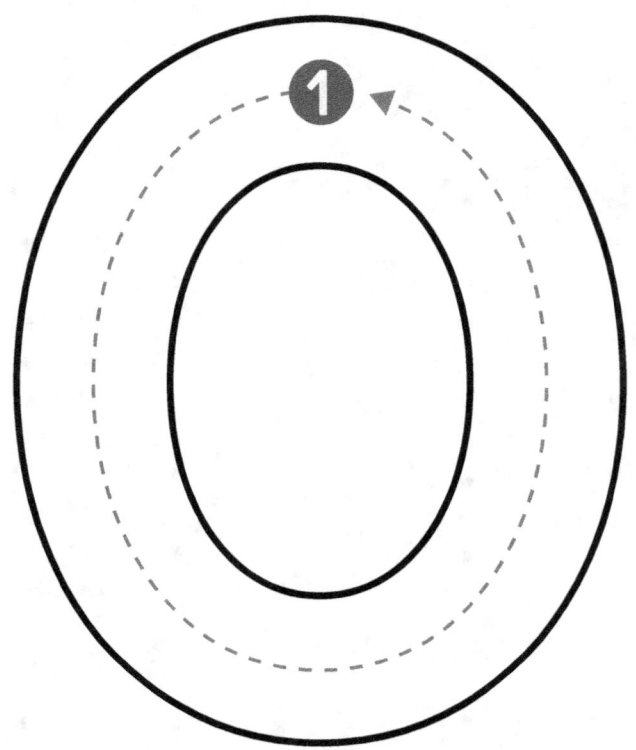

Trace the letters

Finger trace the letter

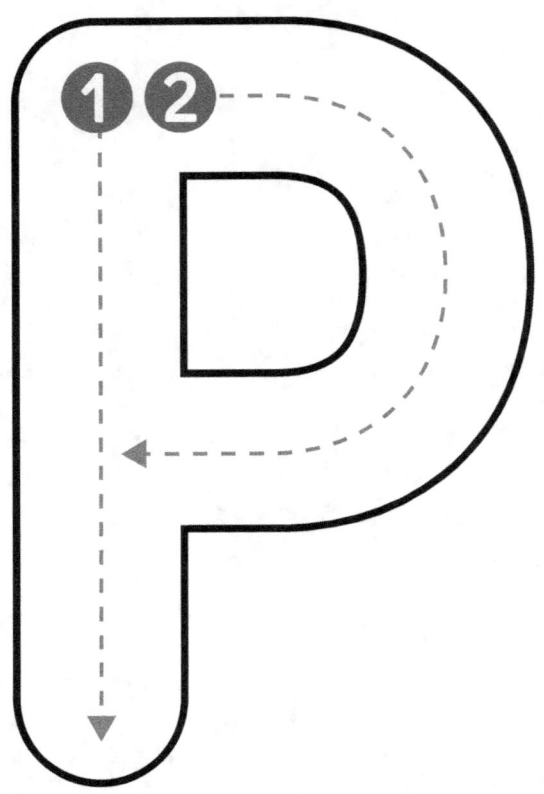

Trace the letters

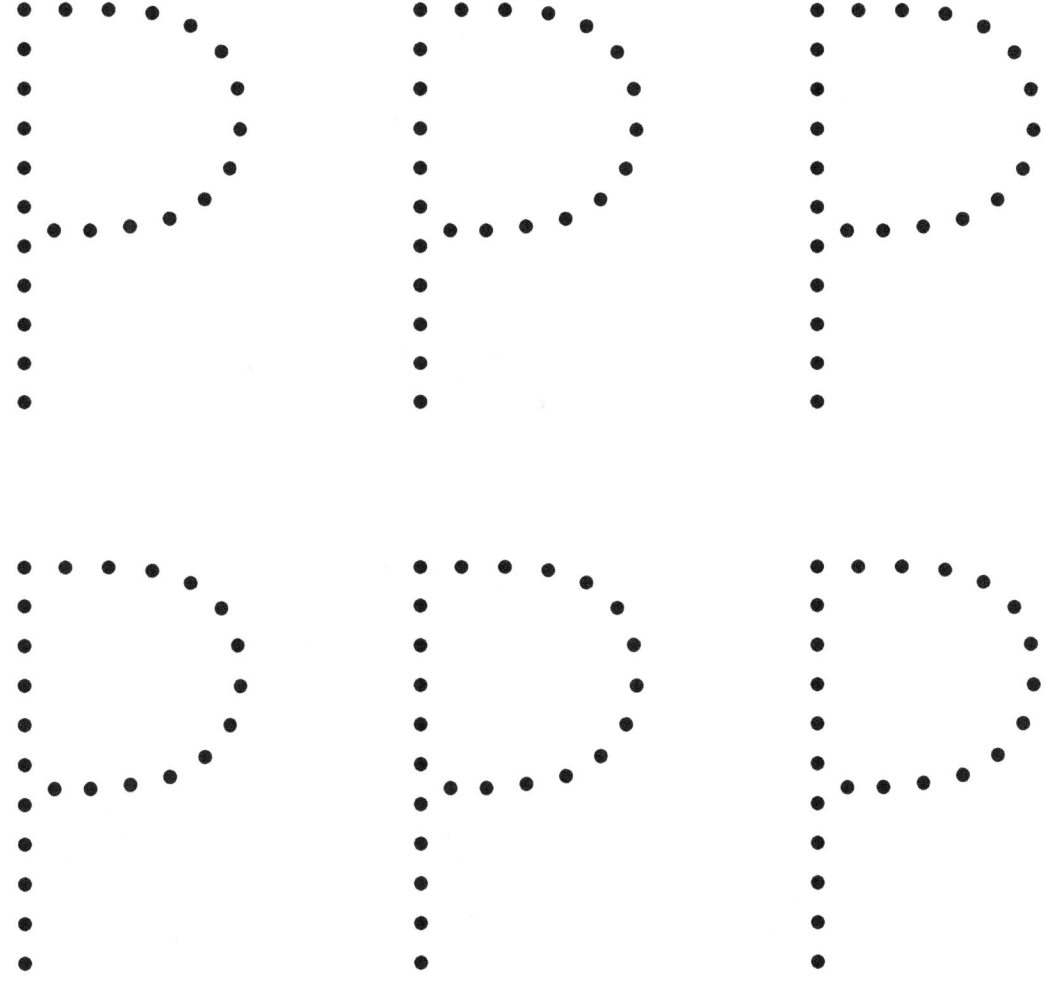

Finger trace the letter

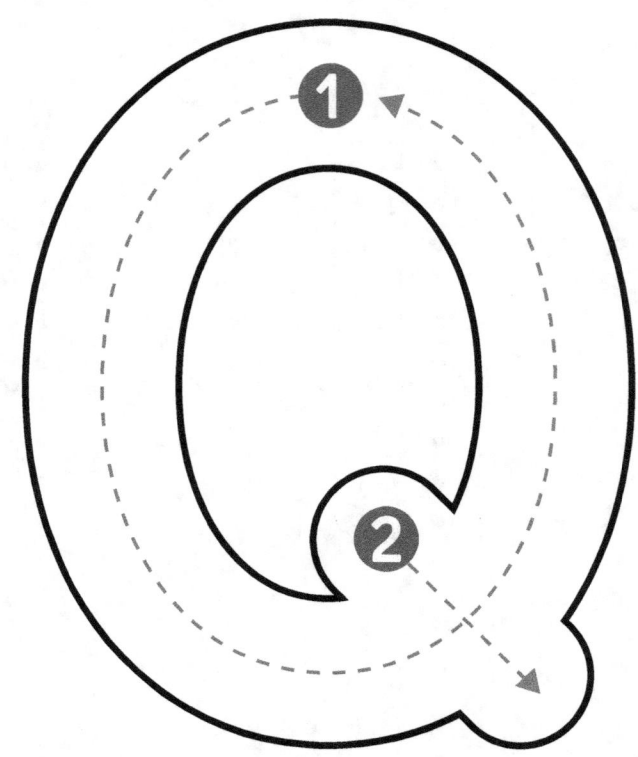

Trace the letters

Finger trace the letter

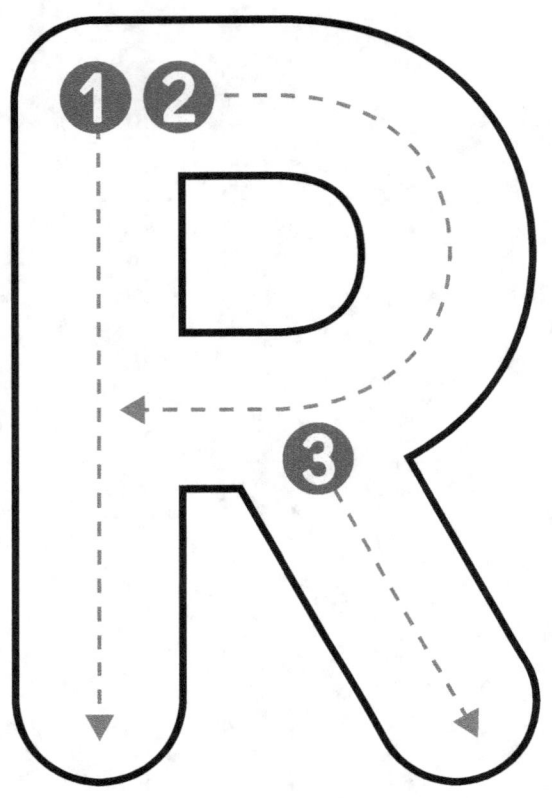

Trace the letters

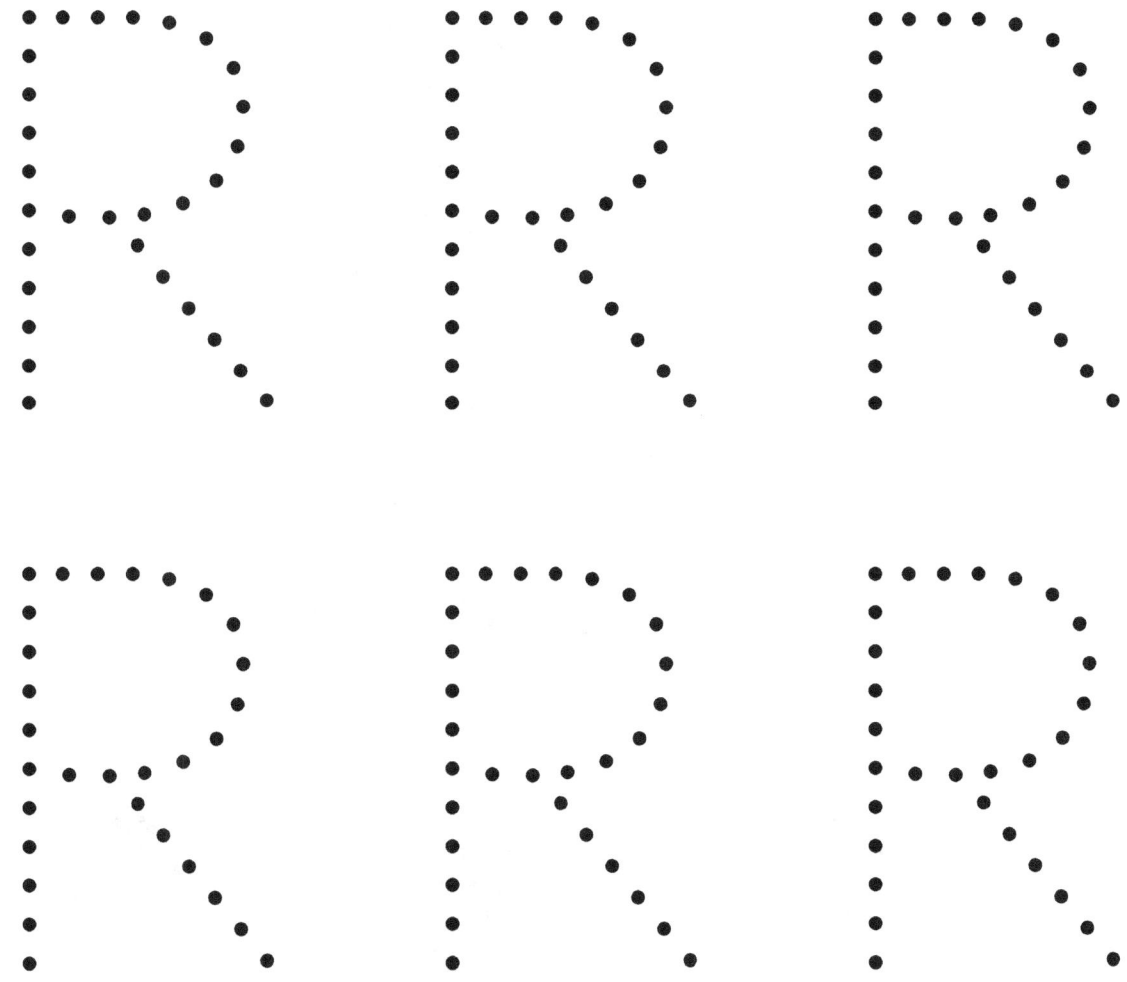

Finger trace the letter

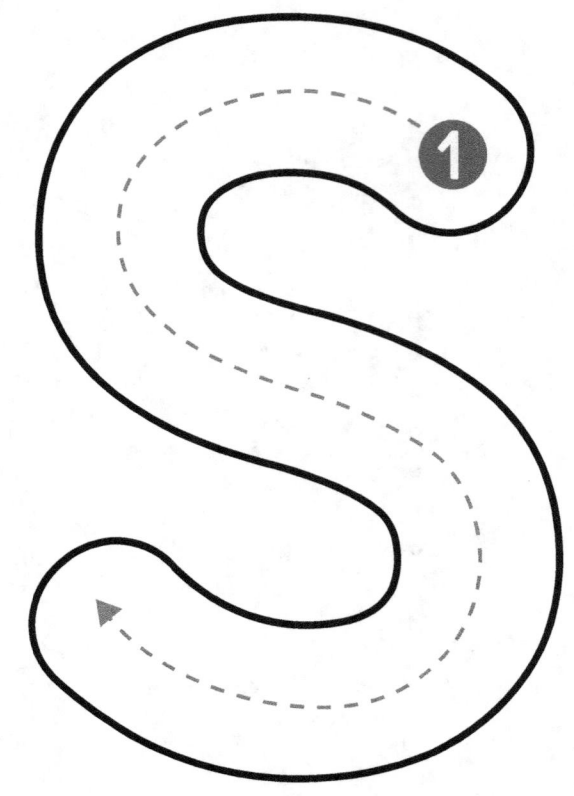

Trace the letters

Finger trace the letter

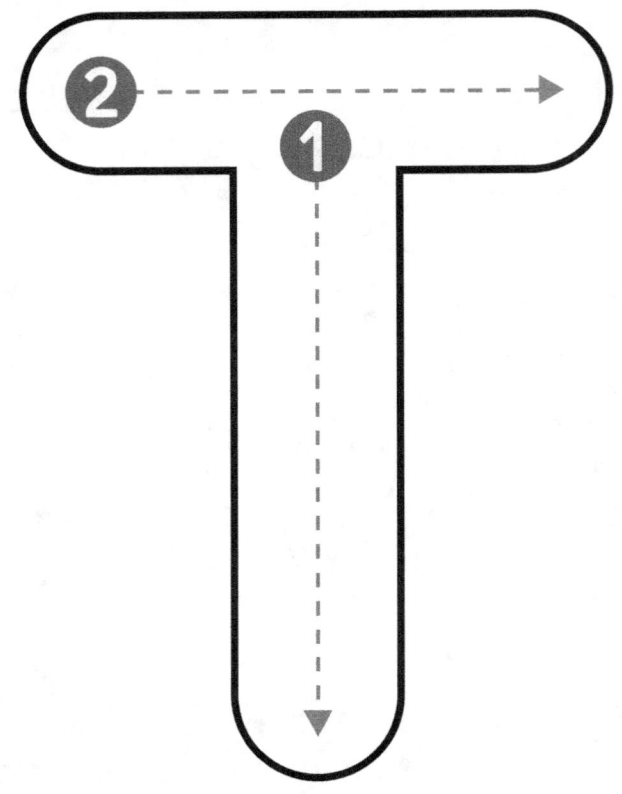

Trace the letters

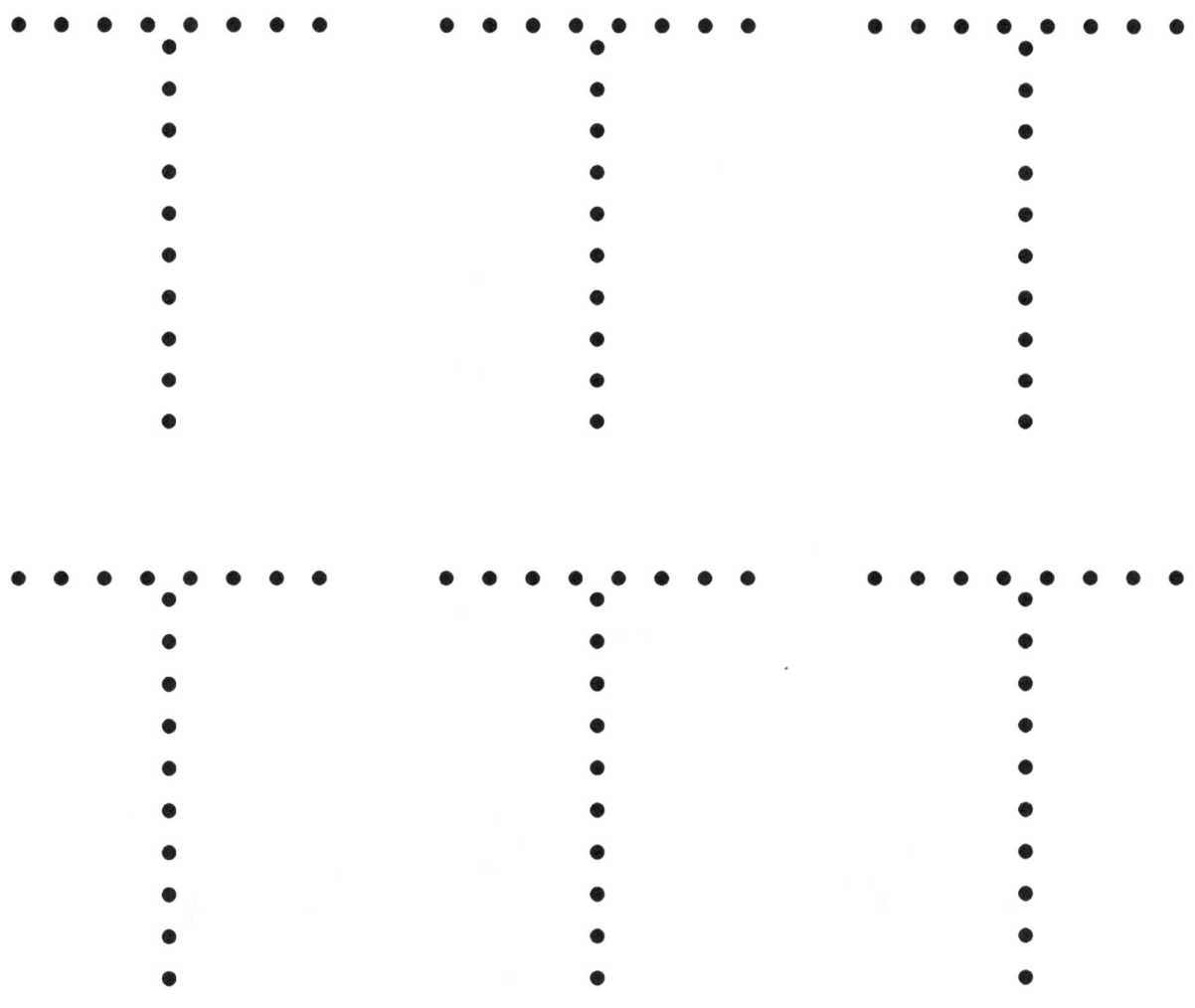

Finger trace the letter

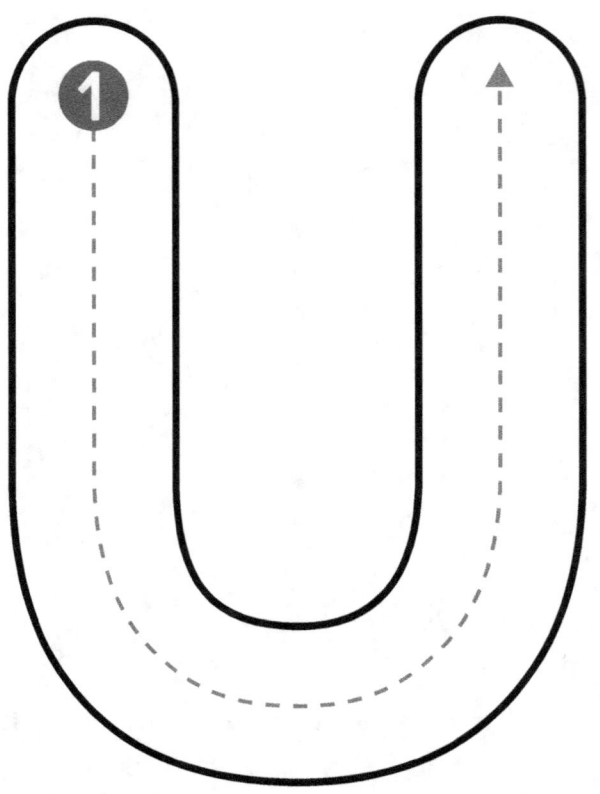

Trace the letters

Finger trace the letter

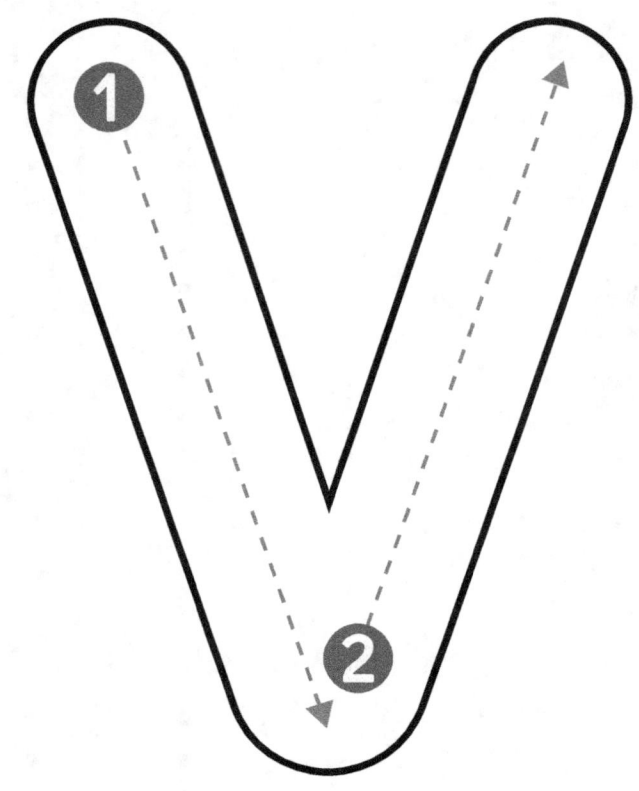

Trace the letters

Finger trace the letter

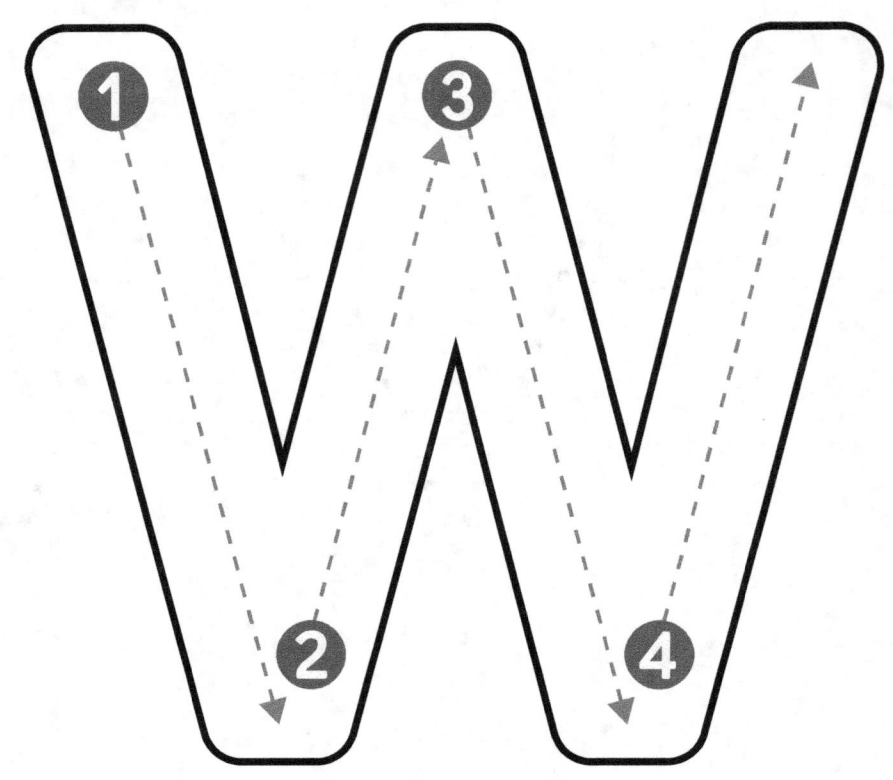

Trace the letters

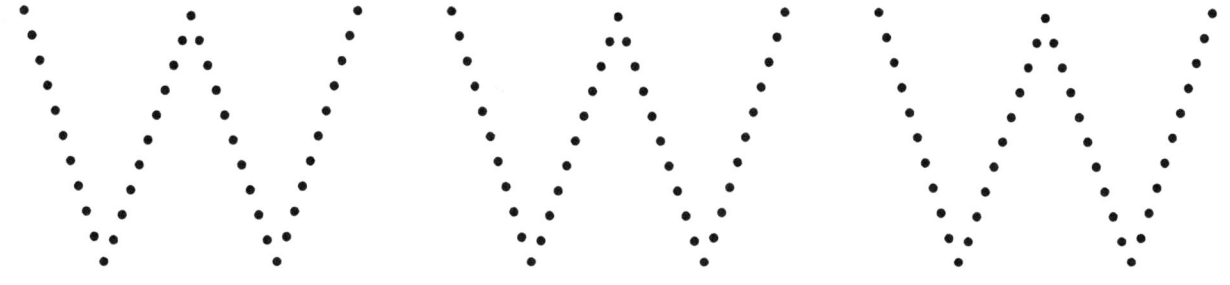

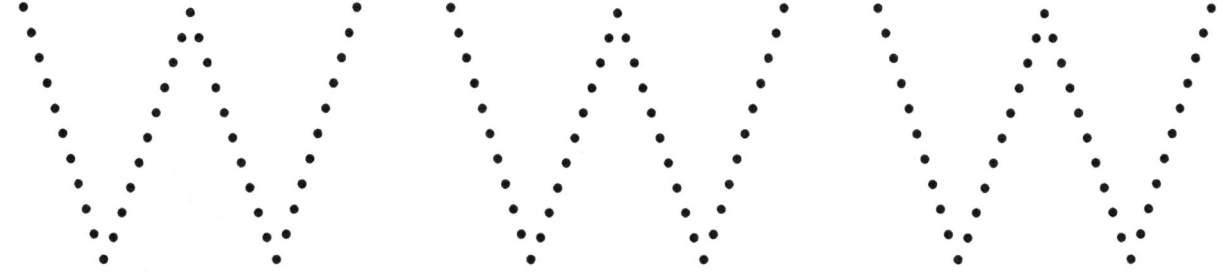

Finger trace the letter

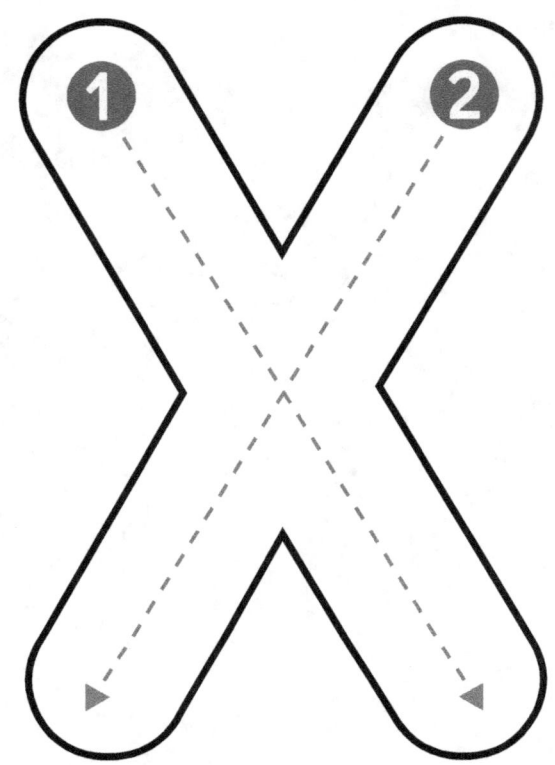

Trace the letters

Finger trace the letter

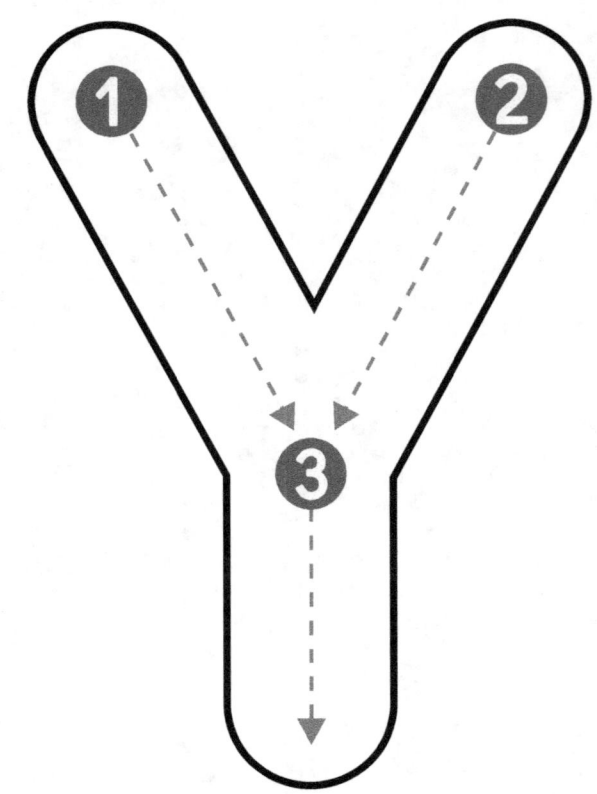

Trace the letters

Finger trace the letter

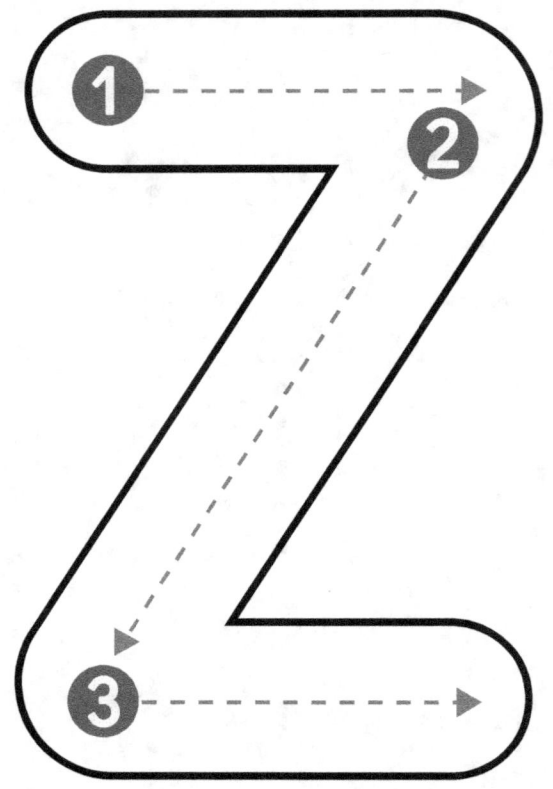

Trace the letters

A B C D E
F G H I
J K L M
N O P Q R
S T U V
W X Y Z

Siohan Scholars presents
this certificate to

for completion of the

UPPERCASE LETTER
TRACING WORKBOOK

Visit siohanpress.com for more workbooks.

www.ingramcontent.com/pod-product-compliance
Lightning Source LLC
Chambersburg PA
CBHW081009120626
46546CB00010B/3078

 Focused on uppercase letters to allow maximum engagement for completion

 Develop fine motors skills with pencil control while following each letter

 Stimulate the different senses by using both fingers and pencils to trace the letters

SIOHAN PRESS
A PUBLISHING COMPANY

ISBN 978-1-959451-99-0

9 781959 451990